FOR

Retold by Claudine Gandolfi

Illustrated by Jo Gershman
Designed by Lesley Ehlers

PETER PAUPER PRESS, INC.
WHITE PLAINS, NEW YORK

Thank you to everyone who stood behind me, sometimes pushing, while I wrote: Mom, Dad, Grandma, Michele, Maria, Jen, Judy, Eva, Latisha, Sheila, Steph, Brenda, Amy, Marie-Hélène, Katie, and Sol.

Illustrations copyright © 1999 Jo Gershman.

Text copyright © 1999
Peter Pauper Press, Inc.
202 Mamaroneck Avenue
White Plains, NY 10601
All rights reserved
ISBN 0-88088-410-X
Printed in China
7 6 5 4 3 2 1

Contents

Introduction • 8

Pwyll and Rhiannon • 10

The Wooing of Etain • 23

Oenghus and Caer • 40

Diarmaid and Grainne • 46

Gawain and Dame Ragnell • 53

Introduction

THE LIGHT AND THE DARK,
GREAT JOYS AND GREAT SORROWS,
"EARTHY" WIT AND MYSTICAL WONDER,
THE PAGAN AND THE CHRISTIAN

Celtic tales are full of paradoxes, and derive much of their power from this fact. They embody the Celtic world view, so different from that of the rest of Western thought, that the pagan and Christian aspects of reality co-exist and each contributes to our understanding of life.

The Celts held their bards in high regard. The more fanciful the tale the more acclaimed it became. Their tales were meant to be heard rather than read, and they have a lyrical, narrative quality that brings them to life. Always romantic in nature, each of these myths brings out the Celtic affinity for joviality, belief in reincarnation, respect for women, and a heightened sense of adventure.

C. G.

Pwyll and Rhiannon

Welsh

The mystical horse-goddess is an image that runs through many Celtic tales. Here, Rhiannon (pronounced Rhee-anne-on), an archetypal horse-goddess, tantalizes her suitor by remaining unattainable and playful. Before she allows anyone to approach, he must recognize her sovereignty. The horsewoman signifies companionship to travelers in times of danger. She is guardian and protector, and clearly represents a guide or link to the otherworld.

Pwyll (Póo-eell), Lord of Dyfed (Dóve-edd), was hosting a magnificent feast at his court at Arberth. After the first course was served, Pwyll felt the need to stretch his legs. He left the court with some members of his retinue, and happened upon the hill known as the Throne of Arberth. Legend had it that when a nobleman sat on the Throne either harm would befall him or he would view a great wonder.

The brave and adventurous Pwyll scoffed at the threat of danger. "No ill

can befall me among so many men. But, to see a great wonder would surely be pleasant." And so Pwyll sat upon the Throne of Arberth.

Suddenly, there appeared a tantalizing woman, dressed entirely in gold silk, riding a powerful gray-white steed. All of Pwyll's men were enchanted by her visage. Her magnificent horse maintained a steady, slow pace until it was almost opposite where Pwyll was seated. Amazed, Pwyll called to his men, "Do any of you recognize this woman?" But not one among them knew who she was.

Pwyll sent his men to her in order to ascertain her name. Whenever any man approached her, the horsewoman rode past him. The quicker the man walked, the further away seemed the woman. Not wanting to be outdone, Pwyll summoned his best riders to mount their fastest horses and pursue her. The harder the men rode, the further away she appeared to be, although she never seemed to vary her speed. Surely, Pwyll thought, some fairy magic was at work here. Pwyll and his men turned back to the court.

The next morning, the men went about their usual chores as if the woman had never appeared. At dinnertime, Pwyll announced that he planned to return to the Throne of Arberth and lay in wait for the

apparition. Sure enough, the horsewoman reappeared. A strong youth under Pwyll's command was sent with his swiftest horse to catch the vision, but the young warrior failed. The horsewoman never changed pace but was never caught. Pwyll determined that there must be a reason for her arrival. She must want something. If only she weren't so obstinate! Dismayed, the king and his men returned to the court.

The following day Pwyll himself saddled his great horse and set off to capture the elusive lady. Relentlessly he pursued her. She eluded him just as easily as she had his men. His horse, lathered and spent, could take no more. Finally, Pwyll called out: "Lady, wait for me! For the sake of him whom you love, wait!"

She turned slowly, "Gladly will I wait. Wouldn't it have been far better for you and your horse if you had simply asked that of me in the first place?" The woman reined in her horse next to Pwyll, and lifted her veil.

"What brings you to the Throne, lady?"

"I have traveled here on my business. I am glad to see you."

"You are a most welcome sight," he said. Even the most beautiful women Pwyll had ever seen paled in comparison to this rider. "Will you tell me

what your business is?"

The woman looked at him as she answered: "My most important business is to see you."

Pwyll smiled, "As far as I'm concerned, that's the best business you could have. Will you tell me your name?"

"I am Rhiannon, daughter of Hefeydd the Old, and I am being forced to marry against my will. I have not married until now . . . because I am in love with you. I refuse to accept any other suitor until I hear your answer. If you reject me, I shall return home."

Shocked, Pwyll gave her an immediate reply. "If I could choose among the fairest maidens in the world, I would still choose you as my bride, Rhiannon."

"Agreed then. You must arrange to meet me before I am given to another man."

"Arrange the meeting. The sooner it is, the better for me."

"One year from tonight, my lord. I'll arrange for a great feast in your honor at the court of Hefeydd the Old."

"I shall be there."

"Remember to keep your word. Farewell," and Rhiannon parted from Pwyll. When Pwyll's men questioned him about his conversation with the mysterious woman, Pwyll never said a word and quickly moved to change the subject.

Exactly one year later Pwyll prepared himself in his finest clothes and journeyed to the court of Hefeydd, where he was welcomed warmly by the aged king and the assembled dignitaries. All who were in attendance celebrated amidst a great deal of food and drink. A young man with auburn hair soon joined the feast and requested a favor of Pwyll.

"Whatever your wish may be, you shall have it," Pwyll said graciously.

Rhiannon's face turned crimson, "Why did you answer like that? In front of all!"

Pwyll was confused by Rhiannon's reaction. "What is it you wish, sir?" he asked the young man.

"I wish to sleep with the woman I have desired more than life itself. I ask for Rhiannon, and for our wedding feast to be celebrated here."

Pwyll was dumbstruck, but Rhiannon reacted quickly. "You had better keep quiet; there was never a more foolish man than you," she said to

Pwyll. "This is the man I was promised to against my will. His name is Gwawl, son of Clud. Now you must give me to him because everyone here has witnessed your promise."

Pwyll straightened himself up and replied, "Never." Rhiannon moved closer to Pwyll so that no one else could hear her plan. "You must give me to him but I will make sure he never touches me. I will give you a small bag for safekeeping. When Gwawl asks you for the feast tell him that it is not yours to give. I'll make arrangements to marry him exactly one year from tonight. When you arrive with your men, dress in rags and carry this bag. Ask for it to be filled with food. The bag is charmed and can never be filled. When Gwawl asks if the bag will ever be full, tell him that a nobleman must stomp down on the contents to make it so. Once he does this, turn the bag upside down, trapping him, and knot the laces. Make sure to bring your horn to alert your men when the time comes to attack the court."

Gwawl grew impatient, "Pwyll, what is your answer?"

"Whatever is mine is yours," he replied.

A year passed. The members of the court and the dignitaries reassembled in the court of Hefeydd, and Pwyll asked that the bag be filled with food.

Just as Rhiannon had predicted, Gwawl grew impatient and asked if the bag would ever be filled. With the encouragement of his betrothed, Gwawl stepped inside the sack and stomped down the contents. Pwyll trapped him in the bag, sounded his horn, and his men attacked the court. Pwyll's soldiers beat the bag with Gwawl in it as if playing a game. He begged for mercy. Rhiannon asked for the beating to stop, and set down the terms for his release: Gwawl had to relinquish all claim to her and the feast in front of witnesses. Gwawl, the defeated usurper, agreed.

Another year passed. Rhiannon and Pwyll had their wedding and exchanged their vows. The celebratory feast lasted many days. This time Pwyll was empowered by Rhiannon to grant favors and gifts to each of the guests. King Pwyll and his new queen returned to Dyfed together.

Pwyll and Rhiannon ruled their country happily and well. However, during the third year of their reign, the people grew sad because their king had no heir. His aides encouraged Pwyll to take another wife, thinking Rhiannon infertile. After all, the king was not growing younger, and stability in the kingdom could be ensured only by the birth of an heir. Pwyll agreed to consider taking another wife if one more year passed without a

son. Before the year passed, however, Rhiannon gave birth to a healthy and beautiful baby boy.

Unfortunately, the six women who were brought in to care for the infant fell asleep on the night that he was born, as did Rhiannon. The women awoke to discover an empty cradle. In a panic, one woman came up with a plan to remove blame from them for falling asleep. They would kill a puppy that had just been born to a hound, and smear Rhiannon with its blood. The six women would swear that, in a fit of madness, the queen had killed her own child. Rhiannon awakened and asked for her son. The leader claimed that Rhiannon had beaten them all black and blue and killed the child.

"Poor woman," pleaded Rhiannon, "there is no need to fabricate this story. Don't falsely accuse me. God knows the truth. If you're afraid of something I will defend you."

The women stuck to their story. News of the disaster could not be kept from Pwyll and the court. Upon hearing of the tragedy, the noblemen sent word to Pwyll to banish his queen from the court as her punishment for murdering the child. The king would not bend to the noblemen's wishes

despite Rhiannon's apparent guilt. Rhiannon summoned the most learned men in her court, and they counseled her to accept her punishment.

The queen was required to stay by the gates of the court for seven years and tell her wretched story to all who entered her kingdom. She was to offer to carry arriving pilgrims on her back, if they would let her, although rarely would anyone allow himself to be carried. This chore, and the sorrow she felt at the loss of her child, were her penance.

Far away, in the kingdom of Gwent Is Coed, a poor man named Teyrnon approached each May Day with fear and dread. Each year on that day, Teyrnon's prized mare gave birth to a foal. Each time the mare gave birth the foal mysteriously disappeared. This year, Teyrnon swore to his wife that he would find out what became of the missing animals. He armed himself and kept watch in the barn. The mare gave birth to a sturdy foal which immediately stood up on its hind legs and pranced around. When he went to examine the foal, Teyrnon heard a loud noise. The claw of a great beast came through the window. Teyrnon struck the claw off between the elbow and the wrist, saving the young horse. He threw open the door and chased the wounded winged creature, but it flew swiftly, and Teyrnon lost

its trail. Teyrnon returned to find a baby wrapped in silk at the threshold of the open barn door.

Teyrnon returned home to his wife and showed her the child he had found. From the manner in which the infant was dressed, his wife knew that the baby was of noble birth. The childless couple decided to keep the boy. The wife convinced the townswomen to say that the baby was indeed hers. The baby was baptized and named Gwri Golden Hair to match his appearance. The wife asked her husband to have the newborn foal trained and given to the boy, and he agreed to her request.

Years passed. One day Teyrnon heard the story of Rhiannon and the baby that she had lost. He tried to find out the time of the child's birth and the circumstances of his disappearance. It became obvious to Teyrnon that the boy he had found in the barn was in fact the son of King Pwyll, and his queen, Rhiannon. Finally, Teyrnon told his wife that they must not keep the child, especially knowing of the punishment of Rhiannon, and her sorrow. His wife agreed. The poor couple anticipated that they would be blessed threefold by returning the child. They would have the gratitude of Pwyll for returning his son and rewards from Rhiannon for releasing her

from her penance, and if the boy grew into a man of honor, he would look upon them with kindness for the care that they had shown to him.

Teyrnon and his wife traveled with the boy to Arberth and there they were greeted at the gate by the disgraced Rhiannon. She begged them to let her carry them into the court but even the child declined to be carried. Teyrnon met with Pwyll who invited the travelers into his hall for a feast. As they sat at their meal Teyrnon explained how he and his wife had come to find the boy and how they had brought him up as if he were their own.

Teyrnon turned to Rhiannon and said, "Here is your son, my lady. The women who blamed you for his death have done you a grievous wrong. Look at him—there is no doubt he is your very own son."

All the members of the court concurred. Mother and son were blissfully reunited. Rhiannon was absolved of her guilt and the boy was renamed Pryderi ("my care") to signify that his return had ended all her grief and suffering. As thanks, Pwyll promised to give land to Teyrnon and defend it as if it were his own. Pwyll also decreed that Pryderi would one day succeed him as King of Dyfed.

The Wooing of Etain

Irish

The fantastical world of the Celts has room for more flights of fancy than any other canon of legend. In this tale, Oenghus (Angus), the God of Love, acts as divine savior for poor Etain, whose life (or lives, as the case may be) is filled with turbulent twists. The theme of forbidden love between mortal and god illuminates the prevailing force of love as well as man's far-reaching ambition. Etain is the unattainable beauty who draws people to her. She possesses an open heart and a caring soul, as well as an iron will.

The god Midir, brother of Oenghus, fell madly in love with a mortal woman named Etain, daughter of Ailill of Echraidhe. Etain's beauty was of such renown that to refer to a woman as being "as fair as Etain" was considered to be the highest compliment. In order to win Etain for Midir, Oenghus was required to perform three fantastical tasks for Ailill. Then Ailill gave her over in marriage. There was, however, an

additional obstacle to be overcome—Midir's first wife, Fuamnach. Jealous of Etain, Fuamnach had the mortal woman transformed into a pool of water, then a worm, and finally into a purple butterfly.

Even in her altered state, Etain was, because of her association with Midir, blessed with some magical powers. She had the ability to hum Midir to sleep and also to warn him of an enemy's approach. Fuamnach was still jealous and sent a powerful wind to carry the butterfly Etain far away from Midir. Etain was swept away into Oenghus's palace. Recognizing Etain, Oenghus constructed a beautiful bower for her, filled with the sweetest flowers, and she lived there for seven years. Oenghus countered Fuamnach's spell by allowing Etain to regain human form during the night hours that she spent with him. But before Oenghus could summon Midir, Fuamnach sent another wind that blew Etain to the far edges of Ireland. There Etain fluttered in the wilderness for a thousand years. On a certain day, the butterfly fell into a goblet of wine being sipped by the wife of King Etar of Echrad, hero of Ulster, and was swallowed. Rather than being digested, Etain was transformed into the female child to whom Etar's wife would give birth. When Midir found out what had happened, he went to seek his love,

undaunted by the passage of a thousand years.

Meanwhile, the king of Ireland, Eochaid (Yo-hee) Airem, held a grand feast at Tara. Newly ascended to the throne, Eochaid proclaimed that he would need a wife. She could not be just a mere woman—she must possess extraordinary qualities that would make her fit to be the queen of all Ireland. King Eochaid's men scoured the land for a maiden of noble birth who possessed unsurpassed beauty and grace. They found the perfect woman in Etain, the daughter of King Etar.

King Eochaid journeyed through the meadows of Bri Leith, and there he chanced upon a maiden who was about to wash her cascading golden hair in the clearest of springs. Her garments were made of fine green silk, and her cloak was the deepest purple. She held a silver comb embossed in gold, which complemented the four golden birds that adorned her basin. As the king approached, he was captivated by her hyacinth blue eyes and delicate skin. She was the most beautiful woman he had ever encountered. The king was sure that this must be Etain, the woman for whom he had been searching.

He questioned her: "Who are you, fair maiden, and where are you

from?"

"Those are easy questions to answer. I am Etain, daughter of the king of Echrad of the fairy-mound."

The king smiled. He had found his future bride. "May I have an hour's dalliance with you?"

"That was my intention when you summoned me," she said coyly. "I have lived here for twenty years, dwelling on the fairy-mound. Nobles, kings, and all manner of men have come to court me. But I have been waiting for you. I have loved you since I was but a small child, unable to speak. Although I had never seen you or heard your name, I recognized you at once."

"That is the best invitation I have ever received," said Eochaid. "I shall make you welcome and all other women I shall leave for your sake. I will live solely with you for as long as you will have me." The bride-price of seven bond-slaves was given to her and she journeyed with him to Tara, where the king's jubilant hospitality was enjoyed by all.

The three sons of Finn—King Eochaid Airem, Eochaid Fedlech, and Ailill Anglonnach—feasted at Tara. It was there that Ailill fell in love with

the unsurpassed Etain. Ailill's wife noticed her husband's gaze following Etain and questioned him about it. He grew embarrassed and could not look at Etain afterwards. After the month-long celebration at Tara ended, Ailill traveled to his brother's stronghold at Dun Fremain. It was at Dun Fremain that he began pining for Etain. He spent a year growing weak with love-sickness but he would not speak of his love to anyone. King Eochaid knew that something was deeply troubling to his brother Ailill.

"How goes it with you, Ailill? You seem ill yet it cannot be very serious since you have been this way for quite some time, unchanged."

"It grows worse both day and night!"

"What ails you?"

"Truly, I wish I knew."

The king grew concerned for his weary brother and had his doctor summoned. Upon examining the patient, the doctor offered two possible causes for his illness: he was either sick with jealousy or smitten with unrequited love. His secret having been guessed, Ailill grew ashamed but would not confirm the cause of his malady.

As fate would have it, it was time for King Eochaid to make his royal

circuit throughout Ireland. He left his wife, Etain, in his stronghold at Dun Fremain to care for his brother Ailill. She was to treat him gently and kindly as long as he lived. Should he die, the king left specific instructions for his burial. He did not expect his brother to live to see his return at the end of his circuit.

Etain visited her brother-in-law each day as her husband had instructed. She tended to him, sang to him, and made sure he had all of his comforts. Finally, she confronted him about his illness.

"What is the matter, Ailill? Your sickness is so great that we are all concerned. If there is anything we can do to help you recover we will do so without hesitation." Ailill thought carefully and at long last he gave her an answer. . . .

Etain continued to visit Ailill each day and she helped him greatly. She spared no expense and wasted no time because her sorrow was deep, knowing that she was the cause of his affliction. She did not love him but could not bear seeing him in such a way. Finally, she told Ailill that she would tryst with him in the house outside the king's stronghold. She would grant his every desire. Alive with anticipation, Ailill could not sleep that entire

night. However, as the time for their meeting grew near, he became tired and unwillingly fell into a deep sleep.

Etain waited for Ailill at the appointed place. There she saw a man approaching who had Ailill's countenance, but she knew it was not he. When Ailill awoke he was wracked with anguish. He had missed the trysting time! He would rather die than live! Etain visited with him and said that she would meet him at the same place on the next day. But, the next day the same fate befell Ailill, and the same man appeared to Etain.

"You are not the man I have come to meet. Who are you and why are you here?"

"It was fitting for you to tryst with me when you were the daughter of King Ailill of Echraidhe. I was your first husband."

"What is your name? I demand it of you."

"It has never been hard to answer to you, Etain. Midir of Bri Leith is what I am called."

"And why did you part from me if you are who you claim to be?"

"Again, it is my pleasure to answer these questions for you. The spells of Fuamnach tore us apart." Midir took Etain's hand. "Will you come with

me?"

She pulled away from his grasp, "No! I will not trade the king of Ireland for the likes of you, a man of whose lineage and family I know nothing."

Midir smiled, "It was I who filled the heart of Ailill with longing for you. I also prevented him from keeping your assignation. I will not allow him to ruin your honor." Midir turned and left Etain in the house by the stronghold.

A confused Etain visited with Ailill. She told him of the man she had met. His reaction only confirmed what Midir had told her. Ailill was cured of the wasting sickness. He was overjoyed that he was no longer ill and that he had not caused Etain to be unfaithful, and he blessed Etain and the stranger. Etain and Ailill agreed that it was fortunate that everything turned out as it did.

When the king returned from his trek, he asked after his brother and was told the entire tale. He agreed that it was fortunate that things happened as they did. While out on his lands, the king happened to meet a young warrior holding a five-pointed spear in one hand and a gem-encrusted shield in the other. He was dressed in the finest garments. His blonde hair hung

down to his shoulders and his eyes were a clear gray. The king did not know him, but the warrior immediately placed himself under the king's protection.

"Welcome to my kingdom, unknown hero."

"Ah, your hospitality is just as I expected it to be. Thank you."

"I am not familiar with your likeness."

"But I know you well!" the stranger laughed.

"What are you called?" asked the impatient king.

"I am not well known. But if you must know it, I am Midir of Bri Leith."

"And for what reason have you journeyed here?" asked the king.

"Why, to play a game of chess with you, of course."

The king brightened, "I am highly skilled at chess."

"I am here to test that skill."

"Unfortunately, young man, the chess board is stored in the queen's apartments and she has not yet risen today."

But Midir came prepared. "I have with me a chessboard that rivals your own. There is no need to bother your queen." At that, Midir revealed an

ornate silver chessboard with gold playing pieces. Precious stones decorated the board and the pouch to hold the pieces was woven in brass chain mail. The board was set up and the men were seated.

"I will not start to play until we have decided upon a stake," said the king.

"What prize do you wish to play for?"

"It matters not to me, sir."

"Very well," answered Midir. "If you win, I will give you fifty gray horses of the finest quality."

Midir went on describing valuable trophies that he would wager, but the king wanted none of it. He preferred the prize to be something that would benefit his entire kingdom. He asked that Midir's people clear away the rocks from the plains, remove the rushes around the stronghold, cut down the forest of Breg, and build a bridge across the moor of Lamrach to allow men to pass freely across it.

Midir agreed to all of it, and then played and lost a game of chess with the king. And so it was that Midir and his fairy-host had to do King Eochaid's will. The king noticed that Midir's fairy-folk did not harness their

oxen with straps over their brows but used wooden yokes. And so it passed that King Eochaid came to be known as Eochaid the Plowman. He spread the use of this method of plowing throughout Ireland. Midir's forces toiled for Eochaid. Each task put before them was completed in a timely manner and was done exceedingly well.

But there was a breach caused by the fairy-folk. A steward of the king was caught by Midir complaining about one of the fairy-workers. Midir, angered at the disparaging talk, went to speak to the king, who welcomed him again.

"Your welcome is what I fully expected. There is nothing that you asked that has not been done. Now I am angered with you."

"I do not harbor any ill will toward you, Midir. What is it you wish? I shall make it so."

"As you say," Midir thought. "Shall we play at chess again?"

"What stakes shall we have this time?"

"Whatever the winner asks," said Midir, who proceeded to trounce the king swiftly.

"My stake is forfeit to you," said the king.

"If I had wished it, it would have been forfeited long ago."
"What is it that you wish?"
"That I hold Etain in my arms and am granted a kiss from her!"

The king fell silent but knew he had to grant this request. He asked Midir to return in one month's time to collect his winnings. The king did not know that Midir had been secretly wooing Etain. He called her the Fair-haired Woman, yet she would not come with him. Etain had insisted that he receive permission from the king before she would go with him back to his home in the fairy world. So, it was all according to plan that Midir lost the original game of chess in order to receive the forfeiture of the second game. Everything had gone as Midir arranged it.

By the appointed date, the king had summoned his best men to protect his stronghold, because he respected the might of the legions of Midir. All the champions of Ireland were stationed inside Tara. Eochaid's fortress had never been so well defended. Everything was shut tight and locked. As Etain was dispensing wine, and as the men were talking, Midir appeared in the middle of the banquet hall. The assembled crowd was amazed by his sudden presence. The king hastily greeted him and gave him welcome.

"This is how I expected you would greet me, King Eochaid," said Midir. "Now let me have what you have promised me. The debt is due, I have given to you everything you asked for; now you must respond in kind."

"I have not yet thought over your request, Midir."

"You have promised me Etain on this day. Those were your words."

Etain blushed with her shame.

"Do not blush," said Midir to Etain, "you have in no way dishonored yourself. I have been pursuing you for well over a year, plying you with the best gems that Ireland can offer and I have not yet touched you. It is not through your actions that I have won you."

"I told you," said Etain, "that until Eochaid willingly grants me to you I would not go to you. If he does not agree, I grant you nothing."

"And I do not grant you to him," said the king. "But he shall take you in his arms anyhow!"

"So I shall," shouted Midir.

Midir and Etain were transmuted into a pair of swans and flew from the palace at Tara. The king scoured the land and destroyed the fairy-mounds, one by one, until he chanced upon the mound at Bri Leith. From within,

Midir sent sixty women all in the visage of Etain. No one could tell which was the true queen; even Eochaid was deceived. He chose Mess Buachalla, Etain's daughter, instead of his own queen. When he realized the deception he returned to Bri Leith and plundered it. Etain finally made herself known to Eochaid and he bore her away back to Tara in triumph.

Oenghus and Caer

(IRISH)

In the lore of Celtic mythology no one "character" did more to ensure that the course of true love ran smoothly than Oenghus Mac Oc. Oenghus, the God of Love, is described as being followed by four birds, representing his kisses, as a sign of his divinity. Avian imagery runs throughout the tales in which Oenghus appears. He played a role in The Wooing of Etain *for Midir and his powers were always utilized to assist lovers, especially those facing impossible odds. This is the story of Oenghus's own quest for love.*

Oenghus had been surrounded by the magical, even at birth. The god known as the Dagda and the goddess Boann concealed their illicit union and Boann's pregnancy from those around them by causing the earth to cease revolving around the sun for nine months. This trick caused Oenghus to be conceived and born on the same day. Because of the unusual circumstances surrounding his birth, Oenghus was infused with

the power of the sun and grew into a wondrous young man shining with the spirit of innocence, love, and virtue.

Thoughts of love preoccupied young Oenghus's mind, but no thought so touched him as one which appeared to him in dream form. For a whole year, he dreamt of one woman whom he did not know. She was astoundingly beautiful (as "dream lovers" tend to be), and each night she would beckon him, and then swiftly disappear before he could reach her. He knew he would love only her and would accept only her as his wife. So obsessed was Oenghus with his dream maiden that he gradually grew more and more distracted from everyday life. All around him noticed that he had become listless and pale, had lost his appetite, and had grown increasingly weak.

Physicians were summoned to determine the cause of Oenghus's wasting sickness. Though Oenghus knew the cause, he would not disclose it. He feared ridicule if it should become known that the great Oenghus had been struck weak by a dream of a woman who had no earthly or heavenly form. At long last, one of the best physicians in the land, Fergne, diagnosed the wasting sickness for what it was—love sickness.

The River Goddess, Boann, Oenghus's mother, set off on a quest

throughout Ireland to search for the maiden who had appeared to her son. Something had to be done to save him. Such a maiden had to exist, and the determined Boann would find her. Her quest took too long for the Dagda, Oenghus's father, who set off on a search of his own. Neither had any luck. Boann summoned her brother, Bobd Dearg, to help find this woman from Oenghus's dream. For one year Bobd Dearg combed the countryside in search of the dream maiden.

Bobd Dearg finally returned with news. The woman in question was, in fact, real. She lived at a lake in Connacht, a known portal to the otherworld, and her father was a Dannan god. Finally, Oenghus learned her name: Caer Ibormeith (yew-berry). Energized by the news, Oenghus traveled to speak to King Ailill and Queen Maeve of Connacht. With intervention from the Dagda, King Ailill and Oenghus tried to set up a meeting with Caer's father, Ethal. However, Ethal refused to meet with them. King Ailill was angered by Ethal's refusal and so sent his soldiers to destroy the fairy-mound where Ethal lived. Ethal would not be forced. He staunchly refused to hand over his daughter to the likes of King Ailill, knowing that her marriage foretold his own death. Ethal made it clear that his daughter's

powers were greater than his; there was fairy magic involved. A show of force would never win her hand. Oenghus would have to find Caer and ask for her hand, and the decision to go with him, or not to, would be hers alone to make.

Oenghus soon learned that his dream maiden lived on Loch Bel Dragon (Lake of the Dragon's Mouth) with one hundred-fifty other maidens. She was a shape-shifter; she was human only every other year, and in alternate years took the form of a swan. Oenghus pleaded with Ethal, who finally told him that if Oenghus truly loved Caer, he must meet her at the lake during the feast of Samhain (SOW-in). During that holiday the link between worlds was stretched thin and he might be able to woo her away.

At the appointed date, Oenghus made his way to the lake in Connacht and he came upon a beautiful vision. The light tip-toed across the swan-laden water and reflected on the silver necklaces of the hundred and fifty swans. The swans were joined two by two by their necklaces. Caer's alone was made of gold. It shone the brightest, and Oenghus beckoned to her.

"Caer! Oh, please come to me."

"Who calls to me?" she replied.

"It is I, Oenghus Mac Oc, and I have loved you in my dreams. I die for love of you."

Hearing his pleas, Caer replied that she would agree to meet with him only in the form of a swan. She would not relinquish her shape-shifting powers for anyone. Oenghus agreed. Invoking the power of his love, he turned the cloak that he wore into wings of the purest white feathers, and he joined her in swan form on the lake. The couple embraced, and three times they glided across the lake singing in unison.

After they were mated, the swans flew to Oenghus's home, Brugh na Bóinne, in Newgrange. Returning to human form, they threw a grand celebration feast for all the land. There was much excitement, fun, and joy that day. Oenghus and Caer graced their guests with a song so beautifully sung that everyone was lulled to sleep for three nights.

Diarmaid and Grainne

Scottish/Irish

Fionn MacCumhail (Finn MacCool), the hero of the Fianna, is the wronged husband in this tale of adulterous love between Diarmaid and Grainne. Grainne, although under the influence of fairy magic, is not the steadfast heroine of the Celts that Deirdre (of the sorrows) is. She is full of life, fears, and desires, and is drawn to the primitive. The God of Love, Oenghus, here intercedes on behalf of these lovers and acts as their protector. As in many Celtic legends, Diarmaid and Grainne *features characters who were once human. The use of shape-shifting in Celtic legend shows a belief in the immortality of the soul. Often, death is not the cessation of life but merely a change. The Celts mirrored this philosophy in their decorative knotwork whose patterns had neither a beginning nor an end.*

Though mortal, Diarmaid Ua Duibhne had Oenghus, the God of Love, as his foster-father. He grew up at Oenghus's home at Newgrange and became one of the most famed heroes of the Fianna. Early in his life, he encountered a fairy woman who touched his brow with her finger, leaving him with a "love-spot." No woman who saw that spot could resist Diarmaid.

The aging champion of the Fianna, Fionn MacCumhail, had decided to marry. His choice was the High King's daughter, Grainne. A great betrothal feast was held and many of the Fianna attended, including Diarmaid. Grainne, however, did not wish to marry the aging hero. She wanted a young husband and began seeking a savior among the gathered guests. Through sheer accident, the hat that Diarmaid wore to cover his "love-spot" came off and Grainne fell under the enchantment of Diarmaid.

Determined to have Diarmaid, the quick-thinking Grainne, before the wedding could take place, drugged the guests with a sleeping potion and placed a *geis* (a request that could not be refused by a warrior without loss of honor) upon Diarmaid. Her *geis* was that he should elope with her. Caught between the proverbial rock (the wrath of Fionn) and a hard place

(the loss of his honor), Diarmaid accepted her *geis*, but with a condition. He would elope with her on the following terms: she must not be on horseback and she could not travel by foot. She must not greet him either indoors or outdoors. Not to be deterred, Grainne met him the following day on a billygoat standing at the threshold of the keep. His condition met, Diarmaid agreed to elope with her, but he refused to be her lover.

When Fionn became aware of Grainne's deception, he grew enraged and revengeful and relentlessly chased the couple for sixteen years. As he neglected his duties as leader, Ireland fell into disrepair and the land fell into near-anarchy. Through his magical insight, Fionn was able repeatedly to locate the couple, but thanks to Diarmaid's foster father, Oenghus, they were always saved. Eventually, Grainne prevailed upon Diarmaid and the two became lovers.

At long last, Fionn tracked the pair to Oenghus's stronghold at Newgrange. Unwilling to allow a battle, Oenghus proposed a truce between the two. They agreed. Diarmaid was finally welcomed as the king's son-in-law and Fionn married another of the High King's daughters. Fionn, however, never forgot the pain that Diarmaid had caused him.

One day, a hunt for the great boar of Ben Bulben was arranged. This was no ordinary boar. Born as the human son of Diarmaid's mother and Roc, Oenghus's steward, the offspring had been transformed into a boar when Oenghus's father killed him. Roc could not bear the thought of his son having died, so he turned him into a mighty boar without hair, ears, or tail. This boar, he decreed, would some day kill Diarmaid—the death of one son, for another.

Diarmaid knew nothing of his misbegotten half-brother until Fionn's invitation to the hunt. Fionn related the history of the beast, and Diarmaid realized Fionn had lured him into a trap. But Diarmaid was not one to shirk his responsibilities. If he was fated to die here, he would. During the hunt he was disemboweled by the boar as he dealt it a death blow.

The mortally wounded Diarmaid begged for assistance from Fionn. There was one thing that would cure Diarmaid—a drink from the hands of Fionn. The hero of the Fianna brought back a handful of water for Diarmaid three times. But each time Fionn remembered what had happened between them and let the life-saving drink trickle through his fingertips.

Diarmaid died, and his body was brought to Oenghus's stronghold in

Newgrange. So distraught was Oenghus that he sent a soul into Diarmaid's lifeless body each day so that he might continue to talk with Diarmaid. Unfortunately, the resurrection could last for only a few moments each day. With Diarmaid out of the way, Fionn ultimately convinced Grainne to become his wife, and they were wed.

Gawain and Dame Ragnell

ARTHURIAN

Dame Ragnell, the "loathly lady" or toothless hag, traditionally symbolized the sovereignty of Ireland and the search for the rightful heir to the throne. Dame Ragnell is tied to the land and extends to the heir the privileges that come with the right to rule. The hag's test of the pretenders to the throne, as well as the true heir, signifies initiation into one's proper place in life, and her horrific countenance tests the mettle of her chosen heroes. Her visage is one that reflects the inner spirit of those who seek to oppose her. This theme of appearance vs. reality runs throughout this tale, beginning with the castle of Tern-Wadling. If you are familiar with Chaucer's Wife of Bath's Tale, *you will see its antecedent here.*

While enjoying the Christmas meal at their castle in Carlisle, King Arthur and Queen Guinevere were hosting their best and brightest champions. The kingdom was peaceful and all were

enjoying royal hospitality on this most joyous holiday. As the members of Arthur's court were well into their celebrations and boasts, caused mainly by an excess of drink, a lone woman entered the hall and threw herself on the ground at the king's feet. She had come to ask for revenge upon a vulgar knight who had disgraced her.

The accused knight had a castle at Tern-Wadling next to a pleasant lake. The battlements were colorfully decorated with streamers, but all was not as it seemed. No knights or ladies could pass through the castle walls without incurring grievous misfortune.

"He's twice the size of an average man and his legs and arms are strong," the woman told Arthur. "On his back he carries a club that is as large as a tree. And yesterday, he took me to the bower and there he forced himself upon me. I told him that I would go directly to you, King Arthur, thinking he'd spare me. But he just laughed and said 'Go tell that cuckold king to meet me if he dares.'"

The king jumped up from his seat and swore an oath across the land. He swore that he would not rest until this vulgar knight was vanquished. "Fetch Excalibur and bring my horse to me," commanded Arthur. "I will

make that wretch regret his loathsome act." When the king came to Tern-Wadling he called from the castle gate, "Come forth you vulgar knight and meet me or else declare yourself my subject."

But the castle was built on magic ground. Whoever tread upon it, no matter how strong and brave, would be made to lose his courage. When the knight emerged ready for battle, King Arthur felt the effects of the debilitating magic. He lost his strength and fell feebly to the ground. The knight demanded that the king meet him in battle or yield his lands. Arthur would be spared only if he returned to Tern-Wadling on New Year's Day, with the answer to the question, "What do women most desire?" If Arthur could not find the correct answer, the vulgar knight would kill him and his lands would be forfeit.

The shaken and disenchanted king swore to return on New Year's Day with the answer, and quickly fled Tern-Wadling. Arthur searched high and low and asked whomever he encountered, "What do women most desire?" Some answered riches, ostentation, or bearing. Others told him joy, or flattery, and some said the company of a jolly knight. The king sent messengers to the far corners of his kingdom with the question enclosed in a pouch.

Each reply he received offered a different answer to the question.

Sorrowfully, he rode across the hills where he chanced upon a woman sitting between an oak and a bush of green holly. She was adorned all in scarlet but her nose was bent and her face was set crooked. Her hair was matted and resembled a nest of snakes writhing upon her head. She had a gray pallor. There was no more wretched-looking woman on earth. She called to the king, but he ignored her calls. "What manner of man are you that you will not speak to me?" she cried. "I may be able to help you even though I don't look seemly to you."

The king felt shame and in his despair said, "If you are able to help me in my quest, I will grant you whatever you wish."

The woman smiled at the king. "Swear that upon the Cross and promise me on your faith, and I will tell you the secret that will pay your ransom."

And so the king made a solemn promise and the lady told him the answer. For her payment, she asked for him to bring to her one of his young, fair, and courtly knights to marry her. Arthur set off to Tern-Wadling with all of his responses. There he was met by the vulgar knight who was ready for battle. One by one he flung Arthur's responses to the ground. "Yield to

me, King Arthur! All of your lands are forfeit to me! These do not correctly answer the question I put to you and shall not save you from death at my hands."

Remembering the loathly lady he met en route, Arthur called out, "I have but one more reply to your question. As I journeyed here I came across a lady sitting between an oak tree and a holly bush, dressed all in scarlet. From her I have this answer: What all women most desire is to have their own will. Now, yield to *me*, you vulgar knight, for I have paid my ransom!"

The knight cursed, "An early death blight her! She that told you this was my own sister, that misshapen hag. I will yield to you as agreed, but this I do vow: If I come across that foul woman, I will watch her burn."

Upon his return home Arthur told Guinevere and the court of the loathly lady whose words had saved his life. But now, his heart was full of sorrow because he must grant this hag one of his best and most courteous knights. "I will go to the loathly lady and I will make her my bride," said Sir Gawain, who was the gentlest knight in all of Camelot. "Do not be sorrowful my king, be joyous. You are saved." King Arthur would hear none of this. Gawain was his nephew and he would not let him marry this

misshapen creature. But Gawain persisted: "I'll marry her for your sake, Uncle. I will be your ransom."

The king knew Gawain's good will and ordered all the knights to accompany him to meet the lady, Dame Ragnell. Any one of them might yet fill Gawain's shoes. They would take hawks and hounds and pretend they were on a hunt. The retinue was filled with the best men in Arthur's kingdom: Lancelot, Stephen, Kaye, Banier, Bors, Garret, and Tristan.

The "hunting party" came upon the oak tree and the green holly, and there saw the lady. She was so brutally ugly that even the bravest of the knights looked away. Kaye could not believe his eyes, and swore under his breath, "Whoever kisses her should fear his own kisses!" But Gawain reminded the retinue of why they had come to her. One of them must agree to be her husband. Kaye laughed—she'd not be a wife of his. The rest of the knights gathered up their hawks and hounds and hastily beat a retreat from the hag. King Arthur commanded his men to stand their ground, but they wouldn't listen.

"Peace, Lords," called Gawain, "there's no need to run in fear. I will take the loathly lady as my wife." Ragnell was so grateful to Gawain that she

promised he would never regret his good deed. The knights took Ragnell back with them and Gawain married her.

On their wedding night, as they lay in bed together, Gawain was struck with panic. "Turn to me, husband dear," cooed Ragnell in his ear. But poor Gawain could hardly bear to lift his head, he was so worried. When he did turn to his wife, he saw not the vile hag, but an exceedingly beautiful and fair lady whom all men would desire. Gawain, amazed at her new-found beauty, kissed his bride deeply.

"The fairest flower is shamed by you, my lady. You cannot be the same woman I married."

"I am your bride, my dear Gawain. I am the same woman that was so lowly and lived upon the moor." Then Ragnell posed another choice for her husband, "Choose wisely, my lord. Do you prefer for me to remain as I now appear by day, or by night? You must choose only one."

Gawain debated the situation with himself. To have her fair in the night would leave all night for play. He'd rather have her foul by day. But, when all the knights and ladies were gathered drinking wine and ale, then he would be mortified, for she'd be unsightly. The situation was impossible.

"Ragnell, I leave the choice up to you because you are my lady and I shall abide by your will."

    Ragnell smiled, "I bless this day and you. Because you left the choice to me I will remain as you see me now, both day and night. My father was an aging knight and he married an evil woman who laid a curse upon me. She banished me to the forest to dwell in that loathly shape as if I were a fiend of hell. Amid the bracken and the bramble I led a lonely existence only to be set free when a fair and courtly knight would make me his wife. I wouldn't regain my own true form unless he granted me my will. She also changed my brother into that vulgar knight. Since the spell is broken by you and her wrongs are now made right, I shall remain your fair lady, and my brother shall become a stately and honorable knight."